The Only Constants

Also by Sarah Agnew and published by Ginninderra Press
On Wisdom's Wings
In Prayer and Protest (Pocket Poets)

Sarah Agnew

The Only Constants

For my many constant friends through this season of change

With gratitude

The Only Constants
ISBN 978 1 76041 114 5
Copyright © text Sarah Agnew 2016
Cover photo: Sarah Agnew

First published 2016 by
Ginninderra Press
PO Box 3461 Port Adelaide 5015 Australia
www.ginninderrapress.com.au

Contents

abiding	7
morning psalm & t'ai chi	9
by the billabong	10
An Ode to Terrible Beauty	11
Unsent Letters	13
walking prayers	18
the only way I know	19
hot water balloon	21
farewell anticipation	22
water fusion	23
unwavering	25
you're welcome	27
Children Cry for Freedom	28
Agnes's story	30
the humble, the great	33
silence	37
peace is a firework	38
given: a meditation on faith	39
What is faith?	41
unrelenting	45
again?	47
insomnia	48
sick	49
Dark Dealer	50
our love	52
the pages' screaming	53
Woe is	55
once more, or twice	56

persevering — 59

- The Hall of Poets — 61
- all the world — 62
- aftertaste of doubt — 63
- in which I ask myself, why did I stay at home? — 64
- to market — 66

change — 69

- only constant remaining — 71
- two walkers and a sleepless poet bear witness… — 72
- dark hours counting — 73
- turning the sandman away — 75
- Christmas Letter — 76
- an unravelling — 79
- sit beside me in my grief? — 80
- unfinished nativity — 81
- Christmas: Present — 82
- having learnt much — 83

abiding

morning psalm & t'ai chi

Psalm 30:5

arms paint the rainbow
kookaburras laughing
scatter night's weeping

by the billabong

a gathering prayer

we gather by the billabong
remnant place of growing
place of deep still
time out from the flow

we gather by the billabong
each one valued
each one needed
in this place,
for this time
out from the river's flow

we gather by the billabong
stirred, unsettled by new water
after rain

we have fallen here, by
the billabong, floated
on wind and water
to this still place of knowing
for a season, for each other

we gather here,
by the billabong, each one
whole with each other
together one
gathered here

An Ode to Terrible Beauty

I love a sunburnt country,
this land, big island red
spread from centre north
and west, east and south
to vineyard's edge, to golden
sands and green blue grey
blue sea –

        to tangled green
of forest and carpet green
of field, I love this land,
this great big island,
its beauty, and yes, its terror.

From spiders in the corners, snakes
in unmown grass, to sting
rays, jellyfish and sharks –
gasp!

        Fires and floods,
cyclones and droughts –
yes, terror lives here too.

And the sun pierces the stark blue sky
with no concern for this brown land's
inhabitants –
we pant, we yearn, we thirst for water.
We thirst for more, for kind
concern from one another,
so rare we hardly dare
imagine welcome for the stranger,
recognition of nations here
first.

This sunburnt land, its sun-
kissed occupants, all
I love; for all I hope –
all nations reconciled who here
are represented, all Aussies
mates, not enemies terrified
of one another – there's terror
enough in our land.

Still, I hope, when all seems lost,
for still, and always, I love
this great big island, my home, my
Australia.

Unsent Letters

1. To: Paul Kelly

cc. Perfect Tripod, The Idea of North

Dear Mr Kelly

I am writing this letter, though I will never send it, to say thank you.

I do not wish to post
the letter to a fan mail address –

I choose not to write this as a Facebook
post or Tweet with the risk of becoming lost
in the crowd.

No, this needs to be a letter, the letter must
be written, a record of my gratitude, though you
will not receive it.

This 'thank you' is for me,
you see – not to me, of course, but for
me. The act of saying thanks an act
of paying attention, to turn my heart
away from fear, toward more love.

So I thank you, Mr Kelly, for your 'Middle
of the Air' – and copy in the a cappella
singers who introduced it to me and so inspire this letter.

When they sing your song, four voices
resounding into the space
                      between –

I let go.

        I fall.

I meet, am met,
        in the middle of the air

and as my feet touch the earth anew I linger there,
and I walk taller, see
more clearly, hear from the re-opened depth
of my own centre.

'Thank you' hardly seems enough,
even this letter less than adequate –

but 'thank you' it is, thank you
I must say, and in doing so I trust
that gratitude
        will resound
    between

2. To: Jane Austen

Dear Ms Austen

It is two hundred years since Lizzy
and Darcy were introduced to the world, and not quite
that long since from this world you
departed; far less time than that since I
first met your characters – met
you

        for you did not leave, not quite
remaining through your words somewhat immortal,
mysterious and hidden behind
living room curtains, in whispers
and manoeuvres, your hand
shown, your heart known a little
in the spaces
        of your novel pages.

I write to you now, though you yourself
will never know it (as far as I know),
to offer thanks, a pause to honour the gift, to pay
homage to a heroine and her heroines,
and turn my heart toward love
once more.

So I thank you: for giving life to Lizzy
and Darcy, Jane and Bingley – to Emma,
Knightly, Fanny; for creating Northanger
and Longbourne, gardens and woods,
picnics on hillsides, wild rides in carriages – did you
ever know what life was begotten by the offspring
of your imagination?

Did these children birthed through pen
offset the pain of absent children from your womb?
Impertinent question, but you will never
hear it to be offended; I ask having found
that I no longer feel regret, the more
word-spun offspring I create – they do
not replace but do take, my love, my care,
attention and set me free
to soar with the Spirit of Creation, in the middle
of the air;

and Jane (if I may be so bold), I hope that you
indeed knew such joy, for joy you did create,
you did beget through the offspring of your pen – and we,
your readers, thank you.

3. To: my one and only love

all of a sudden, my love,
in the middle of it all, you appeared,
beside me, in my face – and my face lit up!
It so surprised me – my smile, more
than the photograph, that I had
to tell you.
        But I will not send this letter; writing
it will honour a moment worth
remembering, a love not quite
forgotten.

There is nothing to regret, you said
to me when I wrote a long-belated
apology for so many other moments missed,
messed up, misunderstood: 'I am grateful for it all, grateful
for you' – I smiled then, too, and dropped
those bulging, ragged bags so I could, this time,
receive your gift.

And here, much later on,
uncovering a treasured memory, I am still
sorry we went our different
ways from there, but free enough to thank
you – thank you – and turn from sorrow
to joy at last at gratitude's
invitation.

walking prayers

1. paying attention

in delight, wonder
I see what variety
God provided wattles

2. attending, prayerfully

as I walk by your house,
the daffodils' bright greeting
almost stops my feet,
and I wonder, do daffodils
mind the bitterness attached
to their sweet beauty
for awareness, remembrance,
cancer's Daffodil Day?

do you feel like pulling
the daffodils out of the ground,
or do the memories not cause you
so much pain?

3. pacing, attentive

I walked past your office yesterday,
when the phone had not yet
pulled your heart through the ground,
when all was still calm,
your father a phone call
away.

the only way I know

for the land that burns in New South Wales, those who live there,
and those who are responding

as the rain falls
and birds discuss the weather
or whatever their tweets
are saying
I paint the rainbow,
greet the moon, and wonder
how to pray today?

how to pray as blue
mountains turn orange-
red, covered with a fiery curtain:

lighting a candle seems crass
somehow, and rudely out of place;
how can I walk when others run, in flight
or toward the fight of their lives?
is there a song I could sing, or music
play to pray away the flames?
would a dance send these clouds
to empty over there, though their gift
is not redundant here?
                       silence

                                 in the face

of tragedy I cannot fathom
only encourages fear – and love
is the better food for prayer.

So I roll the ocean and spread
the wings of the dove and breathe.

When I look up my prayers have been
spoken, and I know they have been received –
though I don't know
                what I said.

Note: 'paint the rainbow', 'greet the moon', 'roll the ocean', and 'wings of the dove' are references to t'ai chi moves.

hot water balloon

or: the day after in the world's hottest city, January 2014

the balloon bursts with fireworks
and bass drum rolls
the thick air seeps at last,
weeps at last into the thirsty earth,
not deep enough to satisfy.
windows breathe release –
freshness in – staleness out –
branches startle with their rude
percussion on iron above.
sweet relief is tainted by bitter fear
as sirens ring out the alarm

farewell anticipation

my eyes caress your slender
silver-cream body, aglow
in winter sunlight, up
and up
        and out along crooked
                              limbs.

your gold-green hair shimmers against
clear kingfisher sky –
        with joy you cry
we are here!

through a eucalyptus shower
do you sense my garbled
gratitude
      or only
            treachery
an odour fouling up the moment
with the promise of foreign thistles?

            I turn my head
dismayed
        and yet
              you stand
tall and strong and with the wind,
you wave me on.

water fusion

rain drops ripple tree
leaves reflection still running
over river rocks

unwavering

you're welcome

if there are no boats sinking,
no one drowning
(for we have stopped the boats);

if there are no parks dying,
no trees to save
(for we have stripped them all);

if there are no rivers drying
up or rising salt
(dam them all!);

if there are no mentally ill,
undereducated, unemployed
first or second Australians
(out of mind the lot of 'em) –

then there is surely nothing left
for us to do but be thanked
(you're welcome):
those of us with all the homes in leafy suburbs,
income guaranteed for life, health
insurance, private planes –
the ones with all the blindfolds.

Children Cry for Freedom

And well may the children weep before you!
They are weary ere they run;
They have never seen the sunshine, nor the glory
much brighter than the sun.
Elizabeth Barrett Browning, 'The Cry of the Children'

Do you hear the children weeping?
On islands far off shore
we cannot see them, lest we see them
for who they truly are – mirrors
of humanity shared with all of us,
creatures as much deserving dignity
we demand, the care and kindness shown
in ready giving to our own kin and kind.

Do you feel the children reaching
heavenward for God? Though the evidence
for God is fading under concrete,
wire, and bars.
                They cling to stories
almost forgotten, songs they know not how to sing
in this strange land of mere existence,
hope of death more promising than life.

Do you know the children, crying,
as you yourself have done? Long
forgotten tears of separation from your mother,
father, home?
                Though you yourself
have never thrown your lot into a boat
of 'illegality', braved the ocean's roar
and fight in flight toward the freedom
of streets that will not explode beneath your feet.

Do you fear the children, calling
for your attention, welcome, love?
Will it challenge your assumptions, or your comfort
far too much?
Can you imagine another running, from a new home
you thought was safe: running, hiding, for
your mates were stolen in the brightness
of the day?
                      This did not happen far away,
but here, among us, and in our name:
we are frightening children and each other,
causing God to weep in shame.

Do you hear the children crying?
Listen. Let them weep.
Join your tears beside them, for they cry
for you, for your humanity,
                      fallen
into the deep.
Can we retrieve it? Will we heal
the broken bonds between us, the soul
of all of us?
Will we heed the children, crying
for their freedom, and the freedom
of us all?

Agnes's story

reading *Burial Rites*, by Hannah Kent

1. The End

Compel her to repent!
Fist pound, sweat drip,
fiery cheek, a premonition
of the witch's stake
she is already tied upon.

Compel her to confess!
Finger point, bold stride,
shout, parry, argue –
prosecute before she's taken
her seat in the dock.

Don't sit beside her, don't let her
speak, don't meet her eye,
I repeat – we know what she
has done and she is through,
swift blade of justice run.

2. Beginning

The young priest hardly knows
what he does as he straps
the harness, hoists up into
his seat, rides towards –
her – condemned, killer, criminal.

'Agnes – may I use your name?'
'That is what it is for.'
And he doesn't say much more.

Needles tapping through yarn break
the silence;
       his eyes rest beside him
on her working woman's hands:

hearth fire and candle glow
warm the room wrapped tight
in winter white; darts flit
forth from dark corners, avoiding
familial targets.

The trapdoor creaks, shy light
seeps through the crack, and one
by one the secrets crawl, released,
into the hungry space between

3. Centre

The platform stands raw
and lonely on the ancient hill.
Witnesses shiver in the sunshine.
Scrape, scrape, the sharpening
of the blade

        thwack!

                she is no lady –

he went first.

Agnes fingers the brooch, the shawl,
gifts of embrace for
a stranger and her story,

eyes held, hands met

and she exhales,

        at last.

the humble, the great

I am
I am he
I am here
I am the one
I am you
I am me
I am come
I am he

I am now
I am ever
I am once
I am always
I am with
I am from
I am come
I am gone

I am with you
I will leave you
I will come
I will be back again
I am here
I am always
I am you
I am he

I am Son
I am man
I am teacher
I am friend
I am prophet
I am trouble
I am come
I am me

I am child
I am man
I am Spirit
I am flesh
I am Wisdom
I am fool
I am Life
I am full

I am neighbour
I am stranger
I am trouble
I am going away
I am come
I am gone
I am you
I am he

I am bread
I am blood
I am betrayed
I am beloved
I am condemned
I am forgiving
I am gone

I am coming again
I am always
I am now
I am life
I am light
I am alive
I am here
I am he

I am teacher
I am friend
I am Spirit
I am life
I am yours
I am God's
I am them
I am us

I am human
I am God
I am Spirit
I am Wisdom
I am here
I am he
I am
I am, friend,
I am with you
to the end

silence

in the still and in the quiet
are we woven, knit and not
the undoing disaster of the loud –
yet noise, do not be silent, your
counterpoint of laughter from the cafe
next door no interruption, passing
traffic no distraction – no,
boundaries you form for our stillness
and our quiet remaking, retying
the frays and stray ends
in friendship with the strangers
lost in war, found in poem,
held in story weaving threads
of life the noise of war will never

peace is a firework

it begins as a whispered possibility
tantalising
frightening
disturbing
then, in a flash of delight –
bursts open
and captures every heart

given: a meditation on faith
drawing on Luke 12 and Hebrew 11

What is faith?

it is a little bit of hope
a little bit of trust
a little bit experience – experience of love
                                  of life
                                  of the Story
                                  of the Sacred Mystery

it's a little bit reaching beyond ourselves
a little bit resting deep within ourselves

it's a bit of belief
a bit of knowledge
a bit ideas
a bit feelings
part tradition
part practice
part attitude
part a way of living

it is mine
it is ours
it is work
it is a gift

faith is a seed that is planted
that we feed and water
that grows
and needs pruning
and care
and love

the writer of the letter to the Hebrews says
that faith is
the assurance of things hoped for, the conviction
of things unseen

trust and hope
experience, belief

faith is a bit like lighting the lamps and waiting
expectantly
for God to arrive;
waiting for an encounter
with the Sacred Mystery who we rarely
see clearly, of whom we catch glimpses
through stories and prayer, song
and love and creation.

faith is a bit like a lamp or a candle – not
much use until it is lit, not much use
hidden under the table.
sometimes ours is the only light, and sometimes
we join a host of candles not only filling
the darkness with light, but warming
us with their combined strength

sometimes the candle burns brightly, sometimes
it flickers in the wind
but we light it
we don't know when we will encounter God, but we hope
and we trust that we will,
for a cloud of witnesses has gone
before us and tells us
that God is here
in the story of the Spirit, Breath, Wind
of God ever stirring; in Holy Wisdom
ever welcoming, God's delight – we see this Wisdom
in Jesus, God made human here with us;
Creation sings its witness to the One
Creator God, Source of life flowing
from Divine Heart of Love.

a little bit of hope
a little bit of trust
experience of love and life,
of Story and Sacred Mystery

some reaching and some resting;
belief and hints of knowledge; ideas
and feelings – a way of life inherited,
shared gift we work to keep alive

faith is lighting a candle in the darkness,
alone or all together,
and waiting
for the Sacred to appear

unrelenting

again?

and despite all efforts,
all resting and sunshine,
all talking and walking and gentleness,
the beast in the corner
still wakes, stretches, yawns –
then leaps
        pinning you down
beneath his hairy black paws
breathing his moist heat in your face
cocking his head in expectation –
        will this time be
the last?
        or can you rally yourself

insomnia

wind and pain
absence of rain
tangled brain

sick

you have been peering through windows
and knocking persistently at the door
finally you have picked the lock and stepped
over the threshold to take me by the throat –

pin me down, take what you want
I am too tired to fight off another cold.

Dark Dealer

Good day, Sir; Madam, good day
to you as well,
come in, and welcome I am sure
you'll find we have most
every shade
of Dark within
and textures, too:

clammy, dripping, deep dank caves
with shafts of light
or none;
velvet purple snuggly coves
for hiding and never being found –
also available in blue –
a tangled jungle,
or the latest in night time desert vastness
with opening and exits or all
closed in;

populated:
we've a wide selection of ghost-inhabited, demon-occupied
Dark,
or shadows
in a smaller range of Dark that come with bonus flickering
candle light;
empty?
we have those, too: Dark
and nothing
but Dark…

special features
include thick brick walls,
trap doors and shackles,
and we have other models
of Dark; you'll see
black dog companions
or grey clouds of Dark
for heart or
        mind

there's a Dark inside
for anyone –

or should I say, my pretties,
there's a human for each of you – don't fret,
don't clamour, no need to fight
over these two here – look,
another just walked in.

ah, madam, you have been chosen,
I see, the velvet Dark
in blue will wear well on you –
and sir – now that
is a Dark
for life

our love

a seed unplanted
branch leaves fruit and flowers
still hidden promise

the pages' screaming

I don't want to read today
this book of friends and faces,
its – woe is mes – and – look
at mes; – its – happy birthdays –
to friends whose birthdays
we don't take the trouble of remembering for
ourselves;
and the reducing of affirmation,
well done you and I agree to
'like'.

    I have had enough
of politics and dogmatics, of
public rants and click and share –
but where
    do we really stand,
or sit, when grief expressed demands
a presence more full than words of sorrow
and regret?

    I would like to close
this book and send a card, see
your face and hold you close;
I desire sand in which to bury
my feet far from news of death
and heartbreak, taste salt, not
bitter pills reissued over and over.

      yet I turn again the page
in hope of someone's 'like' for me –
feed me plastered on the walls
of my enclosure – someone
free me please, disconnect me,
redirect my call,
      to face a friend
in deeper stories told beyond

Woe is

Ugh.
What is this insipid
dribble from my pen,
which has not become, today,
a wand to wave magic
over page, a needle to weave
fabric, brush to paint picture,
complex and beautiful;

I spin only webs, this jumbled
tumbling of metaphor sets
a trap, I trip
on my self-indulgent insipidity –

                      do I cap
it here, replace the lid and stop
the flow of woes and pity
so unpretty? –

                      or do I let it run,
run on through the weak and useless
ink until page and pen resemble

the emptiness
                I feel?

once more, or twice

are you vapour?
are you metamorphic,
transformative; have you
become a shape-shifter
space-sifter – are you a
ghost?

for all the world, it seems
(or perhaps it is only me),
is haunted by you:

only this evening – over supper –
I encountered a thinner-
haired, greyer-bearded
you
        and yesterday
as I set my poems to flight
and gave them breath
on which to dance
I sparked
        curiosity
reignited memory, an old
almost forgotten
longing
        though I did say
goodbye
        didn't I?

you are not here
you never left – for you are
between
every line I pen,
penning myself in;
herded home to the familiar
fantasy by poetry
and memory,
the treasured love for you, hope
for me and you
my undoing
every time I think I'm back
together

persevering

The Hall of Poets

making herself / small / she hovers / by the heavy oak doors /
occasionally / she steps in / that direction / halts
                then retreats / to the shadows /
from inside / the doors open / voices' soft hum / warm haze
fire blaze / enticing / and yet / she remains /
                unmoved / thud / click / stranger's steps
and echo /
                silence /

the stranger returns / halts / hand on door / *hello?* /
                he – / cough / hello /
                     are you a poet ? / ah – /
I want to /
    be /
                well – when you are / come inside /
light / heat / hum thud click /
                silence /
     she trembles / cold / fear / possibility /

and on the next / opening of the heavy oak doors / without
thinking / she jumps in / thud / click / no retreat /

she hovers / in the corner/ watches / steps forward / and back
/ forward / forward / back / in a dance that lasts / forever / so
it seems /

                               until /
                                    close
enough to the table / to be seen / at last / she is /

all the world

I take a bow before
my hidden crowd
                do I hear
in their silence apathy,
or antipathy?
                I was hoping
for applause…
                I bow again
that's your cue, I'm done –
ta daa!

the hollowness illumined
reveals   emptiness
but for one spectator:
                front and centre
Narcissus sits and I
am on the wrong stage.

aftertaste of doubt

elation not shared
soon deflates
toward
        despair
                dejection
much like rejection
                and I
may as well not
have tasted success
                at all

in which I ask myself, why did I stay at home?
on the night of the Light the Dark vigil, 23 February 2014, having
heard Matthew 5:38–48 that morning

was it because it was too hard,
or was it too easy, to light
a candle, hear speeches affirm
your righteous belief in good,
that you did not go to the square
with the others?

was it because of how you are,
fragile, broken easily, no
energy – or is it who you
are, solitary, retreating, or
lazy?

were you overwhelmed, feeling helpless
in the face of so much suffering, so
much cruelty, fear seeming stronger
than love?

was it uncertainty at the purpose,
for one or for all, or do
you not yet know for whom to light
the candle?

because perhaps there is discomfort
at the movement's critique of government
as though 'they' are not also humans
in need of compassion? Sure,
their actions diminish the fullness
of being of the scared
and desperate humans seeking
refuge in our land – and
remove a measure of our humanity
and their own as well

but there is a part of me that wonders
what it would be like to light
a candle for Mr Abbott, Mr Morrison,
the man who pulled the trigger
and those who stood by watching
chaos unfolding on that island
prison camp – could we restore
a measure of humanity, give life,
give love to those we have made
the enemy?

to market

walking through the doors
from cold to steamy sweaty
hall, regret takes her arm
suddenly – she swats it away,
but glances back – is he right?
the other dress, more curls, gloves
in newer style, the safety of home
might all have been better
decisions to make.

                       no.
stay.
        drink.
                sit.
                        wait.

to trust the course and follow through
leaves little energy for conversation,
even observation, which might show her gloves
on the hands of other girls, the curly
styles she well resisted, and the interest
directed toward her.
                      but she feels
unobserved, unnoticed, unwanted,
no hand offered, her hand not requested,
as another dance concludes without her.

and now she feels the heat of a spotlight,
glowing red from within as her odd dress,
plain hair, partnerless adorning of the wall
puts her at odds with all around her imported
unbelonging.
                        perhaps invisibility was better;
she starts to long for a passage home, to where
she is known and need not enter
                                    this fray
of frills and fortune-seeking, sit in a chair not
on a the talent shelf on display, for sale.

change

only constant remaining

when all has changed, remember:
what stays the same is you – and
you are different, too.

two walkers and a sleepless poet bear witness to the morning

they have climbed
Arthur's seat for the moment
the sun will peek
over the horizon as we
turn, and turn, forever
rolling around a universal clock
face, so slowly we don't notice,
so quickly we would like to stop,
for the moment, take the photo,
flash an image to the memory,
press pause, rewind, and play
the moment over in our mind,
when we walked, when we talked,
when we took our time, were not
fools of time or fortune,
hung as if in the middle of the air
and we were there – not coming
and not going, we were there,
and we bore witness to the sun,
to the turning of the earth.
we were there.

dark hours counting

3 a.m.

hour of doubt
what am I doing, mid-thirties,
living amongst teenagers
and twenty-somethings?
it had seemed, on
balance, a good idea, but
at 3 a.m. my first night
here, doors slamming,
feet stomping revellers towards bed
at last, I am not so sure.

4 a.m.

hour of sleeplessness,
muscles protesting
being packed up like cargo
transported across the world;
soul reaching, yearning for Her Holiness
who sent us here,
will I hear you, sing you, praise you
in this strange land? And mind,
for 4 a.m. is the racing restless
hour and thoughts are whirring
past items on the mental check
list – bank account, phone account,
shopping list, and where will I find
the money for all of this?

5 a.m.

the lonely hour
emails from home at once
connect and highlight my dis-
connection, distance from grieving
friends and family football final
rituals
        I have no friends here
yet: I am alone.
I know not the land that holds
me yet: I am not home.
I have spent one day only, no
time yet to set the chords, find
a band with whom to play – I am
playing solo.

6 a.m.

the writing hour
name the fear, write the lists,
with pen on page
shine light into your dark hours,
find your self, your sacred guide,
your hallowed place in poem
tell yourself a story
that will tuck you in
and sprinkle sleep upon your eyes
for one more hour,
and counting.

turning the sandman away

my valued eyes, you are so heavy
with all you've taken in today,
why do you not lay down your burden
in night time's shelter?

my valiant muscles, you are so tight
with all the stretching, climbing,
carrying done today;
let go, let go, recover.

my vigilant mind, you ache
from standing to attention all the long day,
under siege but letting nothing
pass your steady gaze. but nothing
is coming in tonight, slow down,
go back on guard tomorrow.

oh weary being that I am,
blistered toes and heels from walking,
inflamed jaw clamped shut with worry,
numbed fingers from all that writing:
why welcome we not sweet slumber's
emissary, when he taps upon the window?

Christmas Letter

The calendar tells me November
ends tomorrow; Advent then
begins.
I click on the Christmas play
list, slide the everyday
Celtic cross from its silver chain,
slide on the glass Venetian gift
I keep for purple seasons
of waiting. And I wait.

I wait in vain for the sky to turn
to blue from grey as Arthur's Seat
crouches beneath its misty covers,
looking lonely – or is that my
reflection in the window?

I wait for light as I have never
had to wait for it before, winter
followed by winter, naturally,
with the exchange of climate to pay
for dreams. I have heard
that though the heat will rise
in other parts, on this much smaller island
cold and dark and wet will
intensify, so flutter the wings
of butterflies.

I await salvation, liberation,
though I enjoy less, less clarity
and quality of that picture,
for me, at least. Could it be
that my dis-ease is not my own,
but yours and ours together, and I
will be free when we all
sleep peacefully like little ideal
babies in our mangers – an image
so ideal we keep it safely out
of reach, our freedom, though we see
that path to follow.

I wait for joy, for expectation –
celebration – though I have not learnt
how to sing my song in this strange
land, am stranger, am unknown
neighbour, am alone.
                        This matters
here, now, as it has not mattered before,
and I do not know if I will be home
for Christmas, in my dreams or through
the screen, on these streets so cold
and unfamiliar, for home
is but a memory, my seat left
empty with others waiting for my return,
a hope new born of necessity,
since I have flown into adventure.

I wait; for Advent is a season for
our waiting, for blue to turn to gold,
for light in darkest night, for joy to sing
us into life, for hope's embrace
and love's return. What will come
this Christmas, what life be born
through ancient story – I wonder,
as I wait this waiting so unlike
any I have ever known,
waiting,
this year,
with you, alone.

an unravelling

I let go,
drop to the ground,
a light falling, here,
here I will land.
Until now I have been hovering,
wings beat from flying over land
and sea, land and sea, but
land I did not,
feathers panting,
the landing ready
waiting, but landing
had to wait –
for what? an
invitation? the right
one? moments come,
gone, passed over in the hovering
holding height,
watching, moments
wasted waiting
to be ready
to be here
so to come to earth as one,
not fall in pieces,
dreams and ideas scattering
lost with my direction
until now,
when I let go, float
gently to the earth
into breath
to where I am.

sit beside me in my grief?

for Michelle, and her father

I sit in Greyfriar's Kirk and light
a candle with my pen,
listen to wartime Gaelic songs
of lament – I lament,
dear friend, with you
the war your father could not
win, his absence, your
sorrow
Tha mi duilich, duilich,
duilich,
you have sorrow, sorrow,
sorrow
I light a candle in my heart.

Gaelic – '*gah-lik'; tha mi duilich* – '*ha mee doolikh*', meaning I am sad

unfinished nativity

after *The Adoration of the Magi*, Hendrick Goltzius

into the void I pour
empty
despairing
adrift

onto the woman I throw
alone
content
lonely

from the brothers I want
joyful
together
loved

in the light I see
remembered
courageous
hopeful

Christmas: Present

In the bright midwinter, walk we
t'ward the hearth of friendship newly
born here in old Dun Eideann town;
hasten we across the field, on
the city's holy road, with gifts
we come, find sacred gifts abounding –
and laugh we deep and full: aglow
as only folk can be who embrace
the miracles of life, traverse
the sacred paths of light through song
and story old into the heart of hope
with joy and sigh of peace.
And from that hearth we carry now a flame
and float through empty streets of ice.

having learnt much

from Wisdom's fountain,
through pitchers overflowing,
full, life splashes forth

www.ingramcontent.com/pod-product-compliance
Lightning Source LLC
Chambersburg PA
CBHW062147100526
44589CB00014B/1713